BEIJING

a symmetrical city

Written & Illustrated by Dawu Yu

Adapted by Yan Liu

Translated by Crystal Tai

 1 Plus Book

San Francisco, USA

The central axis of Beijing starts from the Forever Stable Gate in the south and ends at the Bell and Drum towers in the north. It is approximately 4.85 miles long. The Imperial Palace, also known as the Forbidden City, is at the middle of the line. Surrounding the Forbidden City are Imperial Walls, which protect the palace. These walls still remain today. During the Qing Dynasty, there were all types of services and supplies for the royal family inside the Imperial Walls. Out side of the Imperial Walls was the Inner City. Then outside the so-called Inner Walls was the Outer City. All these walls were for defense, with gates for people to enter and exit. The walls have since been demolished, and today only their gates are left. .

Now, let's walk through the central axis from south to north to learn about this fascinating symmetrical city.

Fun facts ....

The Yuan Dynasty, built by Mongols, enjoyed more "diversity" than any other era in Chinese history. The urban planning director of Beijing was a Chinese official named Liu Bingzhong, but the chief architect was an Arabian, Amir al-Din.

Knowledge tips ....

Yuan (pronounced as **YOU-en**), Ming, and Qing (pronounced as **Ching**) are the last three dynasties of China, spanning from the mid thirteenth century to the early twentieth century. We know their names are hard to pronounce. However, we will run into them again and again later on, so it'll be better if we take some time try to remember them. "Yuan, Ming, Qing! Yuan, Ming, Qing!" Feel better? Now let's move on.

Layout of Beijing during the Ming and Qing Dynasty

North

Imperial Walls

Imperial City

Outer City

Inner Walls

The Forbidden City

Inner City

Outer Walls

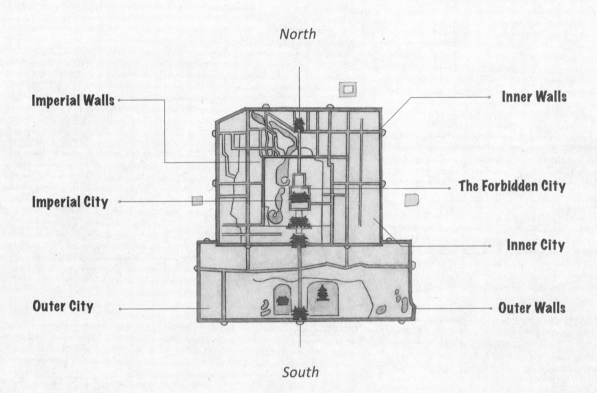

South

The central axis starts at the Forever Stable Gate. It's the southern entrance to old Beijing's outer areas. In the old days, if you lived close by, you'd hear tinkling bells coming and going. Those were camels! The old Beijing relied on camels for transporting supplies. Caravans of camels carried important resources into the city, such as water and coal, right up until the 1950s.

City walls were mainly for defense. Do you see the two rows of windows? Those are arrow slits for soldiers to shoot invaders through. However, because it was too expensive to build around the entire city, the outer walls only shielded the southern end. The Forever Stable Gate has seen many battles happen right in front of it!

From the Forever Stable Gate to the Positive Yang Gate is the outer city of Beijing, which used to be a buffer against invaders. Its walls, streets, and buildings were all lower-quality than those in the inner city. Outer city residents were all commoners, so the area became a center for lower-class business and entertainment, where many stores, theaters, and street performers still present a bustling scene today.

Knowledge tips

The famous Heaven Altar is located in the outer city. Symmetrical to the Heaven Altar, across the central axis, is the Temple of Agriculture. During the Chinese Lunar New Year (a fifteen-day period that starts between January 21 and February 20, depending on the year), the emperor would pray to heaven at the Heaven Altar. During what we now know as early February, which marks initial signs of spring on the traditional Chinese almanac, the emperor would hold a ceremony at the Temple of Agriculture to pray to the god of agriculture for good weather that would result in abundant crops. He would also plow the field outside the temple to set an example for his subjects to dedicate themselves to farm work.

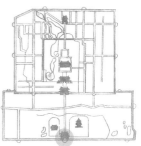

Forever Stable Gate

Let's follow the central axis and go straight north. It will take us to the southern entrance to the Inner City, which is called the Positive Yang Gate. We find ourselves now in old Beijing's business district, where countless shops of every kind are still located. This area is always bustling with activities, but it's even busier and more boisterous when it's close to the Chinese New Year. Look! People are jostling their way through the crowds, busy shopping for the celebration of the Chinese New Year.

The Positive Yang Gate is a very special gate. When it was first built, it had a door on each of its four sides. Horses, carriages, and pedestrians passed through the side doors. The main door faced south and remained closed most of the time. It would only open when the emperor went to the Heaven Altar or the Temple of Agriculture to host ceremonies.

That's why the Positive Yang Gate is bigger and taller than the other gates and designed differently. The Positive Yang Gate is often referred to as the "front gate," now a widely known tourist attraction.

Knowledge tips ....

Above the gate is a gate tower, and in front of that is an archery tower. There was a corner tower at each of the wall's four corners that served as a watchtower for defense. Beijing had a total of forty-seven gate towers, but forty-four of them were removed at different points of time in order to improve traffic. The archery tower we see on top of the Positive Yang Gate today was rebuilt in the twentieth century.

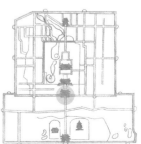

Positive Yang Gate

Across from the Front Gate is the famous Tian'anmen, which means the "Heaven Safety Gate" in Chinese. Between the two gates is the vast Tian'anmen Square, where many national events and ceremonies take place today.

The Tian'anmen is the entrance to the Imperial City. It is one hundred fifteen feet tall. On top of it, Sixty gigantic red pillars support the roof of the gate tower. This used to be where announcements were made, like the emperor's ascension to the throne, his marriage, or other major events. Only the emperor could pass through the main doorway of the Tian'anmen. The moat outside the Tian'anmen is called the Gold Water. There are seven bridges that span across it, all built of jade-like white stone with intricate, beautiful carvings. Today, the image of Tian'anmen is included in China's national emblem, and the Tian'anmen itself has become a symbol of Beijing and China.

Between the Front Gate and Tian'anmen, there used to be a Great Qing Gate (the gate at the bottom of this picture). Do you see the red walls stretching from both sides of the Great Qing Gate and turning toward Tian'anmen? The red

walls surrounded a closed plaza, which used to be an exclusive place for the royal court. Government officials had to get off their horses before entering this area. Commoners were not allowed and would be heavily punished for just peeping in. Along the inner side of the two walls are two rows of central government offices, with officials on the east and military officers on the west. The offices, together with the Great Qing Gate and the red walls, were demolished in the 1950s, so we can freely go anywhere on the Tian'anmen Square nowadays.

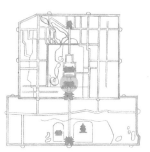

Tian'anmen

Entering through Tian'anmen, we are now in the Imperial City facing the Proper Gate, which resembles Tian'anmen. Guess what's in the gate tower of the Proper Gate? No, there's no weapons there! The gate tower stores ceremonial supplies. When an important ceremony took place, guards of honor lined up from Tian'anmen all the way to the Hall of Supreme Harmony in the Forbidden City, as long as 3,168 feet.

When we face the Proper Gate, to our right is the Imperial Ancestral Shrine, where the emperor prayed to his ancestors. On our left is the Altar of Earth and Harvest, where the emperor prayed every year for good weather that would bring abundant crops all over the country, as well as for stability and prosperity for his people.

In China, ancestors are regarded as gods. The Chinese pray to memorial tablets of their deceased ancestors to show how much they miss and admire them. They also ask their ancestors to keep them safe and make them successful. For the royal family, ancestry was directly related to their right to govern. That's why the Imperial Ancestral Shrine was as important as the Altar of Earth and Harvest, symmetrically positioned across the central axis in the Imperial City.

As we stride through the Noon Gate, in front of our eyes are three halls with red walls and yellow tiles: the Hall of Supreme Harmony, the Hall of Central Harmony, and the Hall of Preserving Harmony. These three halls are the most important buildings. They are the center of the Forbidden City as well as the center of Beijing.

The Hall of Supreme Harmony, which is in the front, is the most magnificent building of the Imperial Palace. It's also the largest wooden structure in China. It was where the emperor ascended to the throne, the empress received her title, and the emperor bid farewell to generals who led troops out to war. The emperor was also congratulated here by government officials on Chinese New Year's Day, the winter solstice, and his own birthday.

Look! What's happening now? What ceremony is about to take place? Everyone is holding their breath and waiting in silence. The emperor is taking a break at the smaller Hall of Central Harmony. In a moment, he will come to the Hall of Supreme Harmony to host a ceremony.

The Hall of Preserving Harmony, which is in the back, is where the emperor hosted a banquet on Chinese New Year's Eve for royal relatives and high officials. It was also where the emperor gave an exam to the finalists of the civil service exams.

Fun facts

When Qing troops took over Beijing, they dismounted their horses in front of the Imperial Ancestral Shrine and respectfully moved the memorial tablets of Ming emperors into another temple, placing their own tablets in the shrine instead. This rite symbolized that the Qing emperor officially became China's ruler.

The cypress trees outside the Imperial Ancestral Shrine are very famous. Most of them are five hundred to six hundred years old. Some of them were planted by Ming emperors.

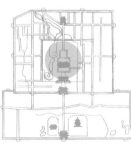

Imperial City

After entering through the Proper Gate, we arrive at the front entrance of the Forbidden City, the U-shaped Noon Gate. In the area in front of this gate, important ceremonies once took place. It was where the emperor announced certain orders and introduced the next lunar year's calendar. It was also where triumphant armies presented captives to the emperor. Ambassadors and local officials gathered here before going to visit the emperor inside the gate.

Just like the Proper Gate, the Noon Gate didn't have any weapons in its gate tower, which stored drums and bells instead. People would hear the drums and bells during important ceremonies.

Between the Proper Gate and the Noon Gate, along both sides of the Imperial Path, there are more than one hundred rooms. Some of them used to be government offices. Others were break rooms for officials to get some rest or review their documents.

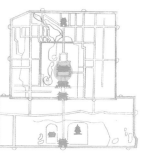

The Three Main Halls

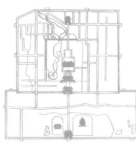

Noon Gate

Let's leave the three halls and continue to follow the central axis north. After entering through the Gate of Heavenly Purity, we are in the place where the emperor, his empress, and his concubines once lived. In the front is the Hall of Heavenly Purity, where the emperor met with high officials, considered policies, and reviewed documents addressed to him. In 1906, the Qing emperor received official letters from Britain and the Austro-Hungarian Empire at this palace. In the back was the Palace of Earthly Tranquility where the empress lived.

Between the two was a path, and along both sides of the path there were courtyards and chambers that were symmetrically positioned. These served as concubines' residences as well as royal tea rooms, royal pharmacies, princes' studies, and Buddhist altars where only members of the royal family were allowed to pray.

Further north is the Imperial Garden. This is where chambers, halls, pavilions, and courtyards are symmetrically placed, dotted by exotic flowers and shapely rocks.

Knowledge tips

It's a Chinese tradition to have the offices in the front and residences in the back. This custom is also required by **The Book of Rites**.

China used to practice polygamy. The emperor had quite a number of concubines in addition to his empress. By contrast, only wealthy men among commoners could afford to marry more than one woman. Polygamy was abolished after the People's Republic of China was founded in 1949.

Fun facts

Following Marco Polo's example during the Yuan Dynasty, more and more European missionaries came to China. They brought many gifts for the emperor. The most attractive gift was a chime clock. On the eastern side of the Hall of Heavenly Purity, there is a room which used to store chime clocks. If you visit the Forbidden City, you will see these items at the clock museum.

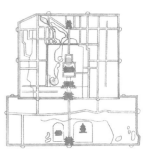

Gate of Heavenly Purity

At the northernmost end of the Forbidden City is Mount Jing, a man-made peak standing two hundred ninety two feet tall. It used to be the highest point of old Beijing. Chambers and pavilions are symmetrically positioned on the hill. From the top of Mount Jing, there is a panoramic view of the symmetrical design of the entire Forbidden City. From south to north along the central axis, all the buildings share the same color scheme and style but differ in size and height. They present a rich rhythm through the neat, orderly design.

Mount Jing was created in 1370 and served as a scenic spot where the royal family went hiking and had picnics. Troops were stationed here during wartime. The last emperor of Ming hanged himself on a tree on Mount Jing when rebels occupied Beijing. Qing troops took the opportunity to defeat the rebels and seized the ruling power of the country. In 1928, Mount Jing became a park where the public can enjoy themselves.

Knowledge tips

Among the Yuan, Ming, and Qing Dynasties, Yuan and Qing were established by ethnic minorities who defeated the Chinese. Yuan was built after the Mongols conquered China. Qing was founded in the northeastern area of China by an ethnic group called Manchu, who took Beijing in 1644 and became the rulers of China. However, the Qing rulers admired Chinese culture. They adopted the culture and political system.

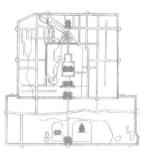

Mount Jing

Let's keep going north and exit through the Earth Safety Gate, the northern gate of the Forbidden City. The ending point of the central axis is the Bell and Drum Towers, which are buildings that used to announce the time. People far away could hear the towers' bell and drum. It helped the commoners schedule their daily work, and the government officials relied on it to get to their morning meetings at the royal court on time.

Around the Bell and Drum Towers, there were many quadrangular neighborhoods with alleys cutting through them. The body of water on the left side of the central axis is the end of the Beijing-Hangzhou Grand Canal. Today, this is called Houhai, which means "Back Sea." It's such a scenic area where many nobles and high officials once lived. Today, the Back Sea neighborhood is where old Beijing's alleys and quadrangular residences are best preserved. This makes it a popular tourist attraction.

Knowledge tips ·

The Beijing-Hangzhou Grand Canal, which is 1,678 miles long, is the world's oldest and largest canal. It connects the fertile farming areas of southeastern China with northern China. During the Yuan Dynasty, the canal was first extended to Beijing. Today, the Grand Canal is a United Nations World Heritage Site, just like the Forbidden City.

Beijing's alleys also date back to the Yuan Dynasty. At that time, narrow streets ran at right angles to one another, forming grid-patterned residential neighborhoods. The narrow streets were later considered alleys and called **hutong** in Chinese. They still remain today and represent Beijing's oldest, most distinctive legacy.

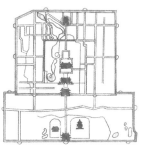

Bell and Drum Towers

Nowadays, Beijing is a 6,490 square-mile cosmopolitan city with a population of 21.7 million. New Beijing does not require a symmetrical layout, but it keeps the central axis to stay true to its heritage. The central axis is protected and preserved. It extends north and reaches where the 2008 Olympics took place. The bird-nest-shaped National Stadium and the National Aquatics Center are symmetrically positioned across the extended central axis. At the end of the extended line is Olympic Park, which is full of lush trees.

With 3,000 years of history, Beijing is one of the oldest cities in the world. It's about the same age as Rome, 1,000 years older than London, 2,600 years older than New York, but 600 years younger than Luoyang, another Chinese city, and 2,000 years younger than Damascus, Syria. Beijing is also one of the world's most populated cities. It's second to Shanghai within China. Tokyo of Japan, Delhi of India, and Mexico City of Mexico also have more residents than Beijing does.

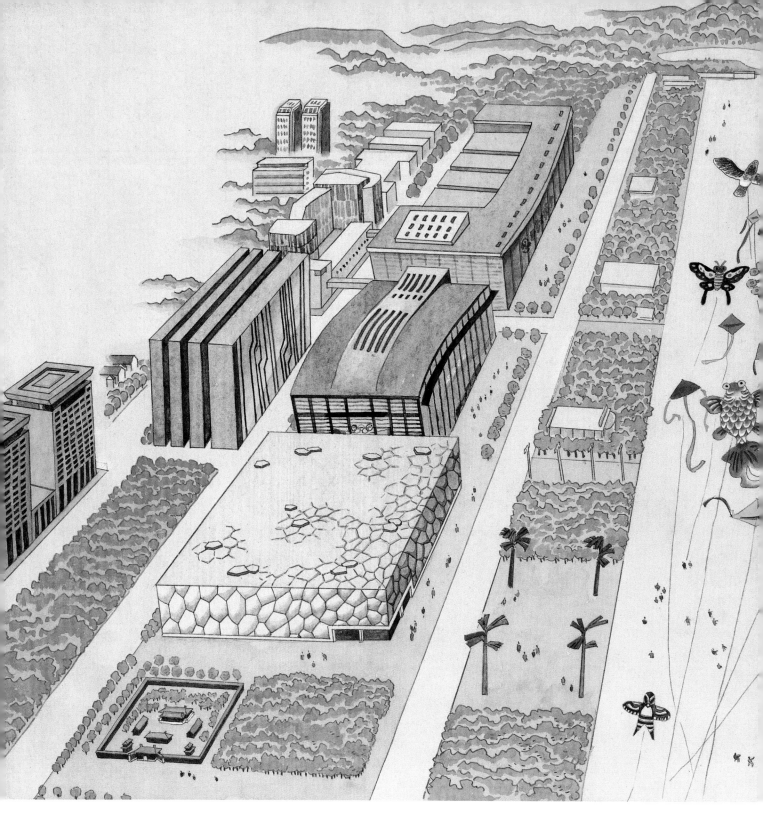

The designers of the "Bird Nest" chose an oval shape instead of the traditional circle to be innovative while staying true to tradition.

The designers of the National Aquatics Center selected a rectangular shape to contrast the oval Bird Nest. The designs of the two buildings reflect a traditional Chinese concept that the sky is a sphere and the earth a square.

Today's Beijing remains a city with a central axis, which connects the south with the north and the past with the present.

Building symmetrical cities is based on traditional Chinese culture. The Chinese value etiquette and order. They believe that order ensures social stability. They also enjoy the harmonious beauty of order and neatness.

| Fun facts |

Including the Forbidden City, Beijing is home to seven UNESCO World Heritage Sites. Can you find out what the other six are? The Central Axis is now on the tentative list of the UNESCO's World Heritage Sites too!

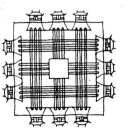

Capital layout as shown in **The Book of Rites**

A Symmetrical City

This book mainly presents how the city of Beijing as it was during the Qing Dynasty (China's last monarchy, 1636–1912). Qing remodeled the city it had inherited from the Yuan and Ming Dynasties. One of the original design principles was the symmetrical layout with a central axis. Qing further developed and perfected the design, making the central axis 4.85 miles long. The city's most important buildings were placed on the central axis.

Now, let's read the map again, starting from the southernmost point of the central axis (the Forever Stable Gate) and going north. Let's appreciate the city of Beijing with its central axis and learn more details about its symmetrical design and architecture.

01

The central axis of the Qing Dynasty's Beijing starts from the Forever Stable Gate at the southern end. Inside the gate, the central axis has the Heaven Altar on its east and the Agriculture God's Altar on its west.

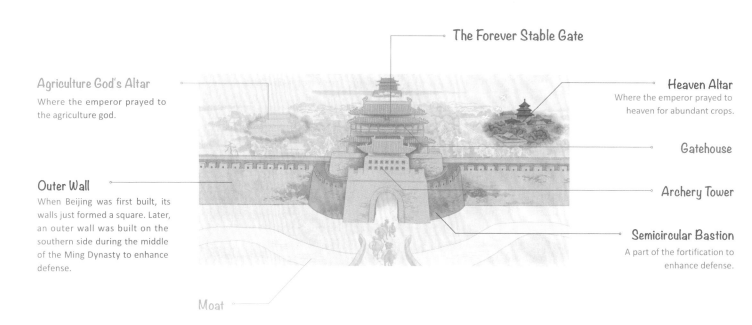

The Forever Stable Gate

Agriculture God's Altar
Where the emperor prayed to the agriculture god.

Heaven Altar
Where the emperor prayed to heaven for abundant crops.

Gatehouse

Outer Wall
When Beijing was first built, its walls just formed a square. Later, an outer wall was built on the southern side during the middle of the Ming Dynasty to enhance defense.

Archery Tower

Semicircular Bastion
A part of the fortification to enhance defense.

Moat

There are many long-established stores near the Positive Yang Gate. The most famous ones include Quanjude Roast Duck and Tongrentang Herbal Pharmacy. They are still widely recognized brand names today. Quanjude is especially popular. Almost every tourist in Beijing goes there to eat the delicious duck they serve.

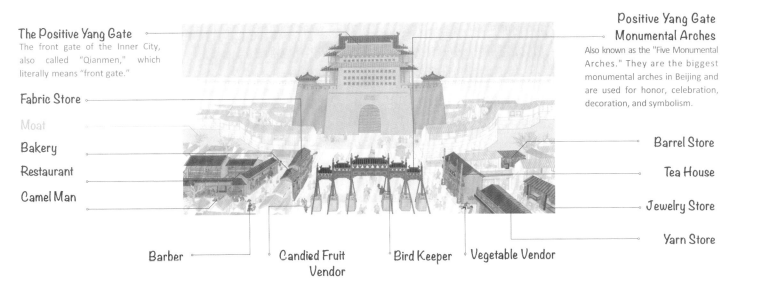

Positive Yang Gate Monumental Arches
Also known as the "Five Monumental Arches." They are the biggest monumental arches in Beijing and are used for honor, celebration, decoration, and symbolism.

The Positive Yang Gate
The front gate of the Inner City, also called "Qianmen," which literally means "front gate."

Fabric Store

Moat

Bakery

Restaurant

Camel Man

Barrel Store

Tea House

Jewelry Store

Yarn Store

Barber

Candied Fruit Vendor

Bird Keeper

Vegetable Vendor

Let's enter the Positive Yang Gate. Then we will face the Great Qing Gate, the southern entrance to the Imperial City, which has the Forbidden City at its center and includes imperial gardens as well as institutions that served the royal family.

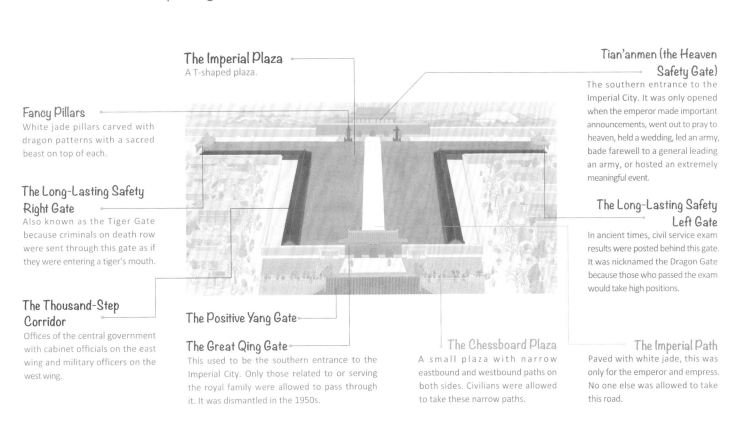

The Imperial Plaza
A T-shaped plaza.

Tian'anmen (the Heaven Safety Gate)
The southern entrance to the Imperial City. It was only opened when the emperor made important announcements, went out to pray to heaven, held a wedding, led an army, bade farewell to a general leading an army, or hosted an extremely meaningful event.

Fancy Pillars
White jade pillars carved with dragon patterns with a sacred beast on top of each.

The Long-Lasting Safety Right Gate
Also known as the Tiger Gate because criminals on death row were sent through this gate as if they were entering a tiger's mouth.

The Long-Lasting Safety Left Gate
In ancient times, civil service exam results were posted behind this gate. It was nicknamed the Dragon Gate because those who passed the exam would take high positions.

The Thousand-Step Corridor
Offices of the central government with cabinet officials on the east wing and military officers on the west wing.

The Positive Yang Gate

The Great Qing Gate
This used to be the southern entrance to the Imperial City. Only those related to or serving the royal family were allowed to pass through it. It was dismantled in the 1950s.

The Chessboard Plaza
A small plaza with narrow eastbound and westbound paths on both sides. Civilians were allowed to take these narrow paths.

The Imperial Path
Paved with white jade, this was only for the emperor and empress. No one else was allowed to take this road.

The Proper Gate is north of the Tian'anmen (the Heaven Safety Gate). Chinese architecture emphasizes harmony and symmetry. The Altar of Earth and Harvests on the west side and the Imperial Ancestral Shrine on the east side have different structures but are positioned symmetrically.

The Altar of Earth and Harvest
This is where the emperor prayed to the god of earth and the god of grains.

The Proper Gate
This has the same structure and style as the Tian'anmen (Heaven Safety Gate). The gatehouse stores flags, umbrellas, and fans, which were used for ceremonies. When the emperor held a large-scale ceremony, guards of honor carried these items from the Hal of Supreme Harmony all the way to the Tian'anmen.

The Imperial Ancestral Shrine
This is where the emperor paid tribute to ancestors. The shrine displays memorial tablets of previous emperors, past empresses, and deceased heroes who made significant contributions to the country.

Tian'anmen (the Heaven Safety Gate)

Not far from the Proper Gate is the Noon Gate, which is the front entrance to the Forbidden City. When there was a morning meeting or ceremony, nobles and officials gathered in front of this gate and then entered through small side doors of the structure, which they were assigned to pass through.

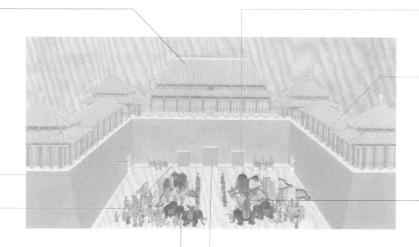

The Noon Gate
This is the largest, classiest, and most magnificent gate of the Forbidden City. In the old days, the Chinese word *wu* (which means "noon") represented the south. The two-dimensional layout of the gate looks like phoenixes spreading their wings, so it is nicknamed the "Five-Phoenix Chamber".

The Right-wing Door

The Right Door
For the nobles

Precious Elephants
Elephants were considered auspicious animals. When there was a morning meeting or ceremony in the palace, elephants carried fancy bottles filled with grains to line up outside. They symbolized peace and abundance.

The Middle Door
Only the emperor could go through this door usually. The empress was allowed to enter through the door on her wedding day. The three people who scored the highest on the annual civil service exam were allowed to exit through it.

The Left Door
For officials and military officers

The Left-wing Door
When the emperor held a ceremony at the Hall of Supreme Harmony, officials and military officers entered and exited through either the left-wing or the right-wing door. The foreign ambassadors did the same.

Fancy Rickshaws
With hoods and wheels, these were used for ceremonies. They came in different sizes and shapes and were made of different materials such as gold, ivory, jade, leather, and wood.

The Forbidden City was divided into the outer court and the inner court. Important ceremonies took place in the outer court at the Halls of Supreme Harmony, Central Harmony, and Perfect Harmony, also known as the three main halls. The inner court was where the emperor lived his daily life.

Hall of Supreme Harmony
Supported by seventy two wood pillars, this is the largest wooden structure still existing in China. The emperor ascended to the throne in this hall. Here he also bade farewell to outgoing armies and was congratulated by his subjects. All the important ceremonies took place here.

Three-tier Platform in the Shape of Mount Meru
Indian legend has it that Mount Meru is the center of the world. Buddhism, which originated in India, brought the idea to China. That's why this platform was meant to be an imitation of Mount Meru. Only the three main halls were allowed to be built on such platforms to emphasize their position at the center of the Forbidden City.

Gate of Heavenly Purity
The front gate of the inner court.

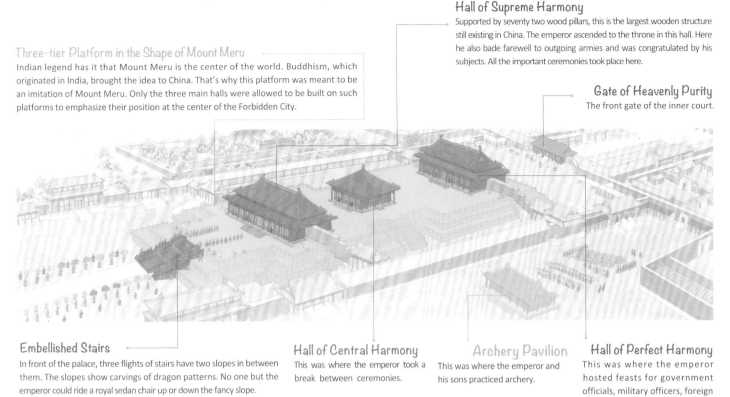

Embellished Stairs
In front of the palace, three flights of stairs have two slopes in between them. The slopes show carvings of dragon patterns. No one but the emperor could ride a royal sedan chair up or down the fancy slope.

Hall of Central Harmony
This was where the emperor took a break between ceremonies.

Archery Pavilion
This was where the emperor and his sons practiced archery.

Hall of Perfect Harmony
This was where the emperor hosted feasts for government officials, military officers, foreign leaders, and religious leaders.

Bronze Crane and Bronze Turtle
Cranes and turtles symbolize longevity. The bronze crane and turtle are actually incense holders. During ceremonies, the smoke of incense came out of their mouths, giving off a sense of mystery.

Yellow Glazed Tiles
Most buildings in the Forbidden City are covered with yellow glazed tiles because the color yellow represents the center in Chinese culture. Only imperial buildings were allowed to use this color.

Dragon-mouth-shaped Lightning Conductors
These two dragon sculptures used to serve as lightning conductors.

Fairy Beasts
These are sculptures of imaginary beasts with auspicious meanings based on Chinese legends. They were initially installed to keep tiles from falling off, but this practical use was eventually combined with wishes for divine blessings. The number of fairy beasts corresponds with the status of the building. Having more fairy beasts on the roof means the building is for higher-class people.

Imperial Measuring Vessel
This measuring vessel was set in a mini stone pavilion, which was placed on top of a white jade pedestal. This was meant to represent the emperor's power in taking measures.

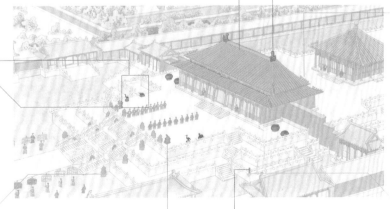

Bronze Incense Holders
There are eighteen of these around the Hall of Supreme Harmony. Each of them sits on top of a white jade pedestal.

Sundial
This device tells the time of day, when there is sunlight, based on the apparent position of the sun in the sky.

Column-top Carvings
The patterns of the carvings represent different ranks. The column-top carvings around the three main halls have patterns of dragons and phoenixes, which indicate the highest ranks.

Dragon-shaped Drains
There are 1,142 of them in total around the three main halls. When it's pouring, all the dragons will spout water at the same time.

07 The inner court was where the emperor, his empress, and his concubines lived. Many historic events and interesting incidents happened here.

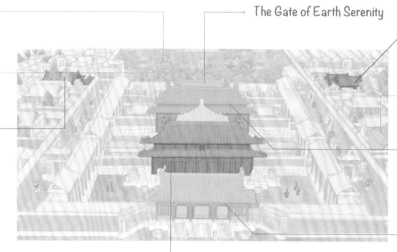

The Imperial Garden

The Hall of Good Fortune
The royal seal of the Qing Dynasty was kept here.

The Palace of Elegance
This is where Empress Dowager Cixi, also known as the Dragon Lady, once lived. She was the most powerful female leader during the last years of the Qing Dynasty. In this building, she gave birth to her only son, who later became Emperor Tongzhi.

The Gate of Earth Serenity

The Palace of Purity
The eighth emperor of the Qing Dynasty, Xianfeng, was born here. He was Cixi's husband and Tongzhi's father.

The Palace of Kindness
The second emperor of the Qing Dynasty, Kangxi, was born here.

The Palace of Earth Serenity
The empress's bedroom was located here.

The Gate of Heavenly Purity
This is the front gate of the inner court where there was tight security. Here the emperor listened to government officials' reports and made decisions.

The Palace of Heavenly Purity
The emperor's bedroom was located here. He also had an office and a banquet hall in this building where he hosted inner court parties.

08 Mount Jing is a man-made hill composed of mud from the moat and the South Lake of Beijing. It was the highest peak on the central axis of the old Beijing. People can get a panoramic view of Beijing on the hilltop.

The Pavilion of Ten Thousand Springs
This is the middle of five pavilions on Mount Jing. It was the highest-altitude building on the central axis.

The Pavilion of One Thousand Autumns
This is located in the middle area of the garden's west side, in a position symmetrical to the Pavilion of Ten Thousand Springs.

Imperial Garden
Rare rocks, exotic flowers, and fancy buildings symmetrically dot the garden. The emperor, empress, and royal family members took a walk, recite poetry, or simply read a book here.

Rockery Pavilion (the Pavilion of Imperial View)
The rockery is composed of rocks of various shapes from Lake Tai in the Yangtze River Delta. The emperor and empress would spend some leisure time in the pavilion on top of the rockery during Chinese holidays in the fall.

The Pavilion of Ten Thousand Springs
This is located in the middle area of the garden's east side, in a position symmetrical to the Pavilion of One Thousand Autumns. Yes, it shares the same name with the one on top of Mount Jing.

This shows what Beijing used to be like in the 1950s. The northern gate of the Forbidden City, The Di'anmen (the Earth Safety Gate), has been torn down. To present the entire original design of the central axis, we painted the gate in this picture.

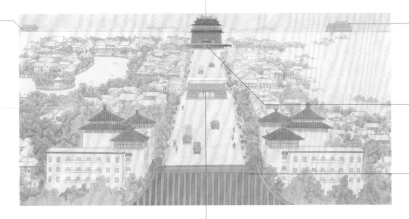

The Bell Tower

The Triumph Gate
One of the nine gates of the Inner City. Triumphant armies returned through this gate.

Shisha Sea
The northwestern corner of the Inner City, where there are three lakes: Front Sea, Back Sea, and West Sea. Temples and historical mansions scatter the area. It preserves the look of the old Beijing better than other places in the city.

The Stability Gate
One of the nine gates of the Inner City. Armies exited through this gate. Dung carts used to go through this gate as well.

The Drum Tower
The drums of the tower used to announce the time every two hours after dark.

The Longevity Hall
This is a replica of the Imperial Ancestral Temple. All the portraits of the emperor's ancestors were kept here. However, it became a youth center from the 1950s through 2011.

The Earth Safety Gate
The northern gate of the Forbidden City, opposite to the Tian'anmen (the Heaven Safety Gate) on the south side. Outside was a business district, which is still boisterous.

The Bell Tower is at the northern end of the old Beijing's central axis, and is about 328 feet north of the Drum Tower. For the 2008 Olympics, however, the central axis was extended north, creating new scenery.

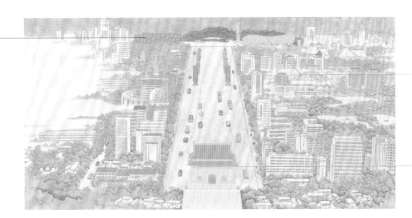

The National Aquatics Center
This was a landmark during the 2008 Olympics.

The Beijing National Stadium
Nicknamed the "Bird's Nest," this was the main location for the 2008 Olympics.

The Bell Tower
The huge bell in this tower used to ring every two hours during the day to announce the time.

Timeline

1046 BC   Beijing is first built.

1153 AD   Beijing first becomes the capital of a kingdom, namely Jin, in China.

1206   Genghis Khan establishes the Mongol Empire.

1227   Genghis Khan dies.

1235   Mongols invade China.

1271   Genghis Khan's grandson Kublai Khan establishes the Yuan Dynasty. Venetian merchant Marco Polo and his father leave Venice for China.

1272   Kublai Khan makes Beijing (called Dadu at the time) the capital of Yuan. The urban planning of Beijing begins.

1279   Yuan troops defeat the last military troops of the Han Chinese and conquer the entire country.

1282   Major buildings of the Imperial Palace and the Imperial Walls are completed.

1293   The Grand Canal is completed.

1368   The Han Chinese conquer Beijing. The Yuan emperor flees north. The Ming Dynasty begins. The Imperial Palace of Yuan is burned down.

1408   The Ming government rebuilds the Forbidden City and the city of Beijing based on the foundation that Yuan has built.

1420	The Forbidden City is completed.
1550	European missionaries come to China again after a gap in time of more than a century.
1626	The Manchu establish the Qing Dynasty in northeastern China.
1644	Rebels within the territory of the Ming Dynasty invade Beijing and burn most of the palaces in the Forbidden City. The Ming emperor kills himself. Qing troops control Beijing. Qing moves its capital to Beijing and rebuilds the Forbidden City.
1695	The new Forbidden City is complete.
1912	The Qing emperor abdicates; the Republic of China is founded.
1924	The last emperor of Qing moves out of the Forbidden City.
1925	The National Palace Museum is established on the site of the Forbidden City.
1949	The People's Republic of China is founded with its capital in Beijing.
1987	The United Nations Organization for Education, Science and Culture (UNESCO) places the Forbidden City on the list of World Heritage Sites.

Glossary

abdicate

to officially give up a position of power or a right

almanac

a calendar based on the Chinese lunar year

altar

a raised table or platform used for religious ceremonies

ambassador

a person who is sent by the government of one country to be its official representative in another country

archery

the sport or practice of shooting with a bow and arrow

arrow slit

a narrow vertical slit in a wall for shooting or looking through

ascension

the act of becoming the emperor

auspicious

likely to be followed by favorable events

bade farewell

to say goodbye to

bastion

a portion of a fortification that projects outward

boisterous

loud, rowdy, and in high spirits

buffer

something that prevents or moderates the interaction of two groups

bustling

moving rapidly and energetically

canal

a channel of water made by humans for transportation or watering crops

central Axis

the main, central part along which other parts are arranged

concubine

a woman who has a social and legal position as a secondary wife

cosmopolitan

including or containing people from many different countries

curator

one who oversees the activities and tends the collections of a building

demolish

to tear down or destroy

dismount

to get down from a horse or vehicle

dowager

the widow of a ruler who retains a title from her dead husband

dynasty

a series of rulers from the same family or group

edict

an order or decree proclaimed by someone in authority

embellished

improved by decorations

etiquette

rules for good behavior and manners

exotic

from a foreign place

harmony

being in agreement and unified

incense

a substance that has a pleasant smell when burned

intricate

very complicated or detailed

jostle

to push, crowd, or bump into

longevity

long life

memorial tablet

a placard used to designate the seat of a deity or past ancestor

Ming

the dynasty ruling China from 1368 to 1644

moat

a deep ditch usually filled with water for protection against enemies

monarchy

a nation or government ruled by or in the name of a king or queen

Mount Meru

the sacred five-peaked mountain considered to be the center of the universe

panoramic

allowing or presenting a wide unbroken view of the surrounding area

pavilion

a light building with open sides

prosperity

the state of being wealthy and successful

Qing

the last imperial dynasty of China from 1636 to 1912

quadrangular

having four sides

residence

a place where someone lives

rickshaw

a light, two-wheeled, hooded vehicle drawn by one or more people

shrine

a sacred place or object that is devoted to some holy person or god

symmetrical

made up of similar parts facing each other or around an axis

Winter Solstice

the date that marks the onset of winter and the shortest day of the year (around December 22 in the northern hemisphere

Yuan

the dynasty ruling China from 1279 to 1368; founded by Mongols

Afterword

By Dawu Yu

In the 1950s, I took painting classes at Youth Palace, located on the northern side of Mount Jing Park in Beijing. The Youth Palace compound comprises a group of historic buildings on the central axis of Beijing. At the center of the compound is a tall building with red walls and yellow tiles named Longevity Hall. I participated in numerous activities in the hall, and I studied art in another building beside it for six years.

In my free time, I often went out with my friends, passing through the southern gate of Youth Palace to climb Mount Jing all the way to the top. That was the highest point of Beijing. From the Ten Thousand Springs Pavilion on top of the hill, we had a panoramic view of the entire city of Beijing. To the south, we saw golden grandeur under the blue sky. The Forbidden City was there. We were able to see the Positive Yang Gate and the outer city. To the north, outside the Earth Tranquility Gate, was heavy traffic and the tall Bell and Drum Towers. I had heard from older relatives that the towers marked the northern end of Beijing's legendary backbone—a central axis.

Decades later, I feel fortunate now about painting the central axis of old Beijing. I am overwhelmed with emotions and memories, perhaps because I have deep feelings for the historic city. I was born in an ordinary alley inside the Stability Gate of Beijing in 1948. When the Earth Tranquility Gate was demolished, my grandfather put me in a cart and brought me there to look at it one last time.

I used to play around the Bell and Drum Towers, Shisha Hai, and the Stability Gate. The bygone glamor of the historic city is etched in my memory. Creating this picture book has served as my emotional outlet along with a more rational analysis of the city's structure. The 4.85-mile-long axis resembles a perfect piece of music, with all the details in precise order to create a glorious composition. To showcase the historical development of the central axis of Beijing, this picture book features three different eras, namely the Qing Dynasty, the 1950s, and the time around the 2008 Olympics, with an attempt to create meaningful content that includes history and modern development.

Historical development always comes at the expense of historic relics. Many historic sites turn into dust and will never reappear. Today's Beijing has gone through drastic changes, but the essence of the city's traditional culture has not been destroyed—and should never be destroyed. It is my duty to present history with my paintbrush and pass on my cultural inheritance to young readers.

Dawu Yu is a Beijing native who grew up in the alleys near the Drum Tower. Later on, with a career dedicated to comics and book illustrations, he won numerous illustration awards, including the Original Picture Book Award from the Asian/Pacific Culture Center for UNESCO in 1988. He was also selected to take part in The Bologna Children's Book Fair Illustrators' Exhibition in 2000. Today, he lives with his family in his beloved city of Beijing.

Yan Liu is a veteran publisher, writer, and translator. She has won multiple national awards for her publishing work in China, including the National Library's Wenjin Book Award. Her recent translation work, the Penguin Guide to the United States Constitution, *was published in Beijing in 2016. Yan moved from China to the US in 2014 and founded 1 Plus Books in the next year to continue pursuing her passion for books.*

Crystal Tai was born in Taipei and moved to San Francisco as a teenager. She earned her master's degree in Education Policy from Stanford University in 2007. Since then, she has worked as a news reporter for local media outlets, a translator, and also a host for a bilingual talk show on local TV. Her most recent work, A Poetic Portal to Chinese Culture, was published in the US in 2019.

Bibliography

Looking Back at Beijing: a Collection of Past Images (回京返照集) by Beijing Cultural Relics Preservation Team. People's Fine Arts Publishing House, 1987.

Historic Images of Old Beijing (回京史照) by Hu, Peiyun.
Beijing Publishing House, 1996.

Lin Huiyin's Speeches on Architecture (林徽因讲建筑) by Lin, Huiyin.
Shaanxi Normal University Press, 2005.

Architecture of the Forbidden City (紫禁城建筑) by Zhou, Suqin.
Forbidden City Press, 2006.

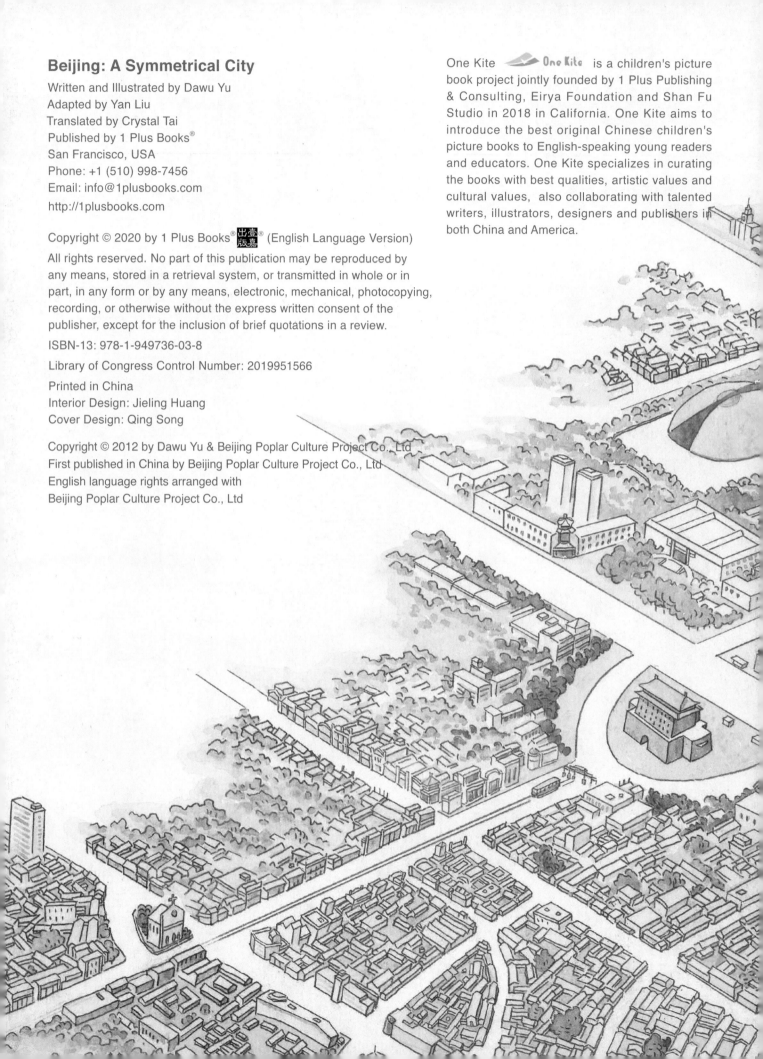

Beijing: A Symmetrical City

Written and Illustrated by Dawu Yu
Adapted by Yan Liu
Translated by Crystal Tai
Published by 1 Plus Books®
San Francisco, USA
Phone: +1 (510) 998-7456
Email: info@1plusbooks.com
http://1plusbooks.com

ISBN-13: 978-1-949736-03-8

Library of Congress Control Number: 2019951566

Printed in China
Interior Design: Jieling Huang
Cover Design: Qing Song

One Kite One Kite is a children's picture book project jointly founded by 1 Plus Publishing & Consulting, Eirya Foundation and Shan Fu Studio in 2018 in California. One Kite aims to introduce the best original Chinese children's picture books to English-speaking young readers and educators. One Kite specializes in curating the books with best qualities, artistic values and cultural values, also collaborating with talented writers, illustrators, designers and publishers in both China and America.